Journey to a Fresh Start

Releasing the Junk....
Revealing the Jewels

By
Janice G. Pettigrew

Journey to a Fresh Start

Releasing the Junk....
Revealing the Jewels

Copyright 2009

Library of Congress Number: TXU00646170

Contents

Dedication

Writing this book has been a labor of love. It has also provided me the opportunity to again marvel at the goodness of God. Without him I am nothing. And I thank him for those persons who have helped to mold and shape me.

First to my dearly departed parents James C. (passed June 1, 1996) and Jewell Gates (passed June 14, 2006), who taught me what they knew and helped me to the very best of their ability.

To my brothers, Jimmy, Ronnie & James and my sister Terrina thanks for just being you. Thank you to my darling angels David and Dion for letting the house stand and growing up to become responsible & loving sons, husbands and fathers. Continue to look out for each other.

I want to say to the founding members of the Fresh Start for Women Board of Directors, Netania Smith, Donna R. Shaw, Keisha Bassett and Sharon Battle, thank you for believing in the vision. Thank you to Ms. Bettye Ferguson who has been with me every step of the way and for giving me the opportunity to act in your plays. To Mr. & Mrs. Charles T. Allen and Mr. & Mrs. John O'Brien thank you for your unwavering support.

Most importantly, to my wonderful husband Oscar. I'm glad I finally gave in and got to know you. It wasn't easy for either of us. I know we both had to learn to trust again. Your love, support and encouragement have been a blessing to me. I love you.

Introduction

In 2003 God gave me a purpose and a mission. Naturally, like many before me I balked. After all, who was I except a mere mortal with faults and flaws for the whole world to see? "Exactly", said God. I carried this around for several months as if it were a baby, waiting to be birthed into the world. Now, as I reflect upon it, that's exactly what it was.

I thought back to when I was pregnant with my first child. The changes my body took me through were at times frightening and at other times it filled me with wonder. As my body grew to accommodate the life I carried inside I found that I was changing as well. I became protective of this human being I had not yet met. I began to plan for its future as if my planning could prevent him or her from experiencing some of the not so pleasant sides of life.

The closer the time came for my child to enter the world the more inadequate I felt. Could I really be a good mom? Would I know what to do? I had a little experience to fall back on. You see, when my youngest brother James was born I was 12 years old and treated him as if he was my baby. I bathed him, changed his diapers, fed him and played with him. Taking care of him was a little different than being responsible for my sister and two other brothers. When they got in trouble I got in trouble!

There are 3 trimesters in pregnancy culminating in the birth of a child. There were 3 phases to my doing God's purpose and mission culminating with the birth of the purpose and mission God gave me.

In the first trimester, there's morning sickness and emotional swings from joy, panic and a sense of wonder and amazement that your body is carrying a small being growing inside you.

In the second trimester many women say they've never been healthier than during this time. This can be attributed to the mother's need to ensure a healthy baby by making healthy choices regarding food, exercise and any other positive outside influences. Suddenly the body begins to exhibit outward signs of the life growing inside.

In the third trimester the body transforms even more as it expands to accommodate the growing baby. Now you're experiencing backaches and other late pregnancy symptoms. As the baby prepares to be born your body sends you a signal. You know the one that may have you bowled over in pain. The trip to the hospital takes forever and why can't someone give you something for pain! And what pain, no one told you it would be that bad! When the doctor examines you and finally tells you to get ready to push, you grit your teeth and bear down with all your might. In your head you're promising yourself that you're never, ever do this again. But then the nurse is placing in your arms that beautiful baby boy or girl and the tears of pain turn into tears of joy. Your most precious jewel has entered the world!

In comparison my life experiences have equipped me to do the purpose and mission God gave me. Like pregnancy I have gone through stages. The first stage was my formative years from birth to adolescence. The second stage, (growing pains) include my teen years and early adult years; many of those years had me in the valley (times of trials & tribulations). The third stage brought me to releasing the junk in my life. This meant examining my life, taking lessons from it all but leaving behind anything that would cause me to not believe in myself. This final stage allowed me to reveal the jewels in my life and bring forth the most precious jewel of all.

Phase I – The Formative Years

Chapter 1 – The Journey Begins

I am a native Georgian, born and raised for the first eight years in the small country town of Pine Mountain by my parents James and Jewell Gates. For those of you who have never heard of Pine Mountain, if you can find your way to Callaway Gardens you've found my hometown. I'm the oldest of five children, I have 1 sister and 3 brothers; and even though my parents moved to the BIG City when I was eight I have always considered myself a country girl. This probably explains why I bought a house in a part of Ellenwood, which still has remnants of the country life. The rooster crows every morning in the neighborhood and in the spring I can sit on my porch and hear the birds singing and watch the squirrels scramble up the trees. The usual city sounds are almost non-existent. Oh and the country girl in me really comes out when it rains, I simply love the rain. The sounds the rain made from my childhood, (it was clink, clink, tinkling sound of the rain falling down on the tin roof of the house and hitting the window panes) always soothed me and sent me fast asleep to dreamland.

My parents each played different but important roles in molding me during my formative years. They instilled in me the desire to be more than what society said I could be. They taught me to be honest, respect others and to work hard for what I want. Take mama. Like most country girls, mama put me in the kitchen at an early age. Thus began my education in learning to cook and if I say so myself, I'm a great cook!! If you love down home country cooking, that's me! Of course my passion is baking. I think this has a lot to do with the fact that mama had me in the kitchen helping to bake my own birthday cake when I was 5 years old. Everyone loved it, at least, that's what they all said.

Another passion of mine is reading. I love to read! It's nothing for me to start on a great book on Saturday morning and not put it down until I've turned the last page, which usually means I'm getting ready to go to bed that night. I love murder mysteries but I'm just as content to read a book for its educational value. My passion for reading I got from mama. I can actually be in a crowded room, find a corner and immerse myself in a book. No I'm not anti-social; I just love to read!

It was mama and not school who sat me down and gave me the talk when I was 10 years old. I didn't totally understand what was happening to me. Imagine playing on the swings at school and some boy telling everyone you'd hurt yourself because blood was running down your leg. I was embarrassed and scared and ran all the way home. Mama made things a little clearer but then she left many things a mystery. I think this was in part because it was the same way with her mama. That day mama introduced me to Kotex and the belt. She taught me how to use it and then she told me I was becoming a young lady and as such I had to behave a little differently.

Suddenly, I was a big girl and was responsible for my sister and brothers. I cursed (under my breath), the day I became a young lady. It was in that talk that mama warned me to keep my legs closed, and to not let little boys touch me down there. But she didn't tell me about the CRAMPS!!! There were other lessons I learned from mama, but those came in later years. I remember her always working always striving for more.

That was the complete opposite of daddy. Daddy was content with a simpler life. We moved to the city not because he wanted to but because mama said we could do more in the city. Years later when they divorced daddy returned to the country.

Growing up I was always a daddy's girl. Up until my late twenties daddy could do no wrong, even when he had to discipline me. You know what I mean back when parents didn't get in trouble for corporal punishment.

Of course in my little girl's eyes, daddy was my hero. It's because of daddy that I love baseball and especially the Braves. Daddy and I were Braves fans long before it was popular to be one. Daddy worked really hard in the fields' back then and he worked even harder when he moved his family to the city. As a result the only past time he had was watching baseball on TV. He never saw a game in person; but that didn't keep him from loving baseball. I was of course too young at the time to understand it all, but to sit and scream and clap and moan with him over a particular play gave me the biggest thrill. I was 15 when Hank Aaron broke Babe Ruth's home run record and daddy and I jumped up and down like we'd just won a million dollars. How many 15 year-old girls do you know that would be watching baseball with their dad? Like I said before, I'm a daddy's girl and he was MY daddy, I just loaned him to my brothers and sister.

It never seemed truer, than during baseball season. When the Braves won the World Series in 1995, daddy was living in New York, but it didn't stop us from talking about our team. And we weren't sad when they didn't repeat in 96', we were still very proud. Keep in mind that I said I love baseball not that I love to play baseball. Believe me there's a huge difference.

Christmas of 1996 brought daddy from New York to spend time with all of his children; everybody competed for his attention. Not me, though! I knew that before the evening was over he and I would find a corner and talk baseball and of course I was right! While in town, daddy made it a point to spend one night with each of his children. When he spent the night at my house I was in seventh heaven. It was only after daddy went back to New York that my brothers, sister and I found out that he'd been diagnosed with cancer. It had already progressed to the point that the doctors could do very little for him. Having been given just 6 months to live, daddy expressed a desire to come home to be closer to his children, so arrangements were made to bring him back to Atlanta to live with my brother and his wife. In January 1997 they flew to New York and brought him home. Though daddy lived with my brother Jimmy and his wife Nancy I made it a point to either call or visit with him every day during the week and every weekend I spent it with him. Being there not only relieved Nancy and Jimmy of some of the responsibility for his care but I got to spend time with daddy that was all mine.

Once the baseball season started I took advantage of every opportunity to watch a game with him. Sometimes we'd watch silently, not really paying attention to the game but enjoying the moment that was just ours. In those moments it was as if we'd gone back in time and I was a kid again.

The last three months of daddy's life had brought us full circle to our favorite time of the year. I'm grateful to God for giving us time with daddy before cancer had him totally bedridden and racked with pain so bad that it was unbearable sometimes to witness. And I'm especially grateful for the moments we shared talking baseball.

The last game daddy and I watched together, the Braves lost. I remember daddy saying "that's okay they'll do better tomorrow," but tomorrow didn't come for him. He died the next day June 1, 1997. Even though I was a girl I think daddy was grateful that one of his children shared his love of baseball. And oh how he loved baseball! That love he passed to me. Every year during the baseball season, do I need to tell you where you can find me? I didn't think so! Just look for me in front of the TV watching and loving a game I can't play. And you know what! Sometimes it feels as if daddy's watching the game with me!

The relationship between my parents had an impact on my relationships. It's through witnessing their struggles, trials and triumphs that I first began to learn how males and females relate to each other. Some of their interactions left me confused and bewildered, especially when there were disagreements. Early on I grew to hate and avoid confrontation. This was due to how I saw my parents handle conflict. More times than not discussions led to raised voices and physical violence.

As much as I loved them both I also feared them. I wanted them to be proud of me and I wanted them to love each other. My parents divorced a year or so after I got married. Each was happier for it, even though they fought and had disagreements we kids still wanted to see our parents together. I believe it was this desire that played a role in my remaining in marriages longer than I should have.

We are a product of our environment in many ways. The important thing to remember is that we can always make changes in our lives regardless of the type of upbringing we had. It all depends on the character you have. I've seen people who never knew their father become great fathers. I've also seen the opposite. In the end we all have to make decisions about our lives. Many times circumstances will force our hand. You can't be on the sidelines and watch life. You have to live it. This is a lesson I've learned.

My parents weren't perfect. Whose are? But they taught me lessons that have played a role in shaping the person I am. Mama was the one that planted the desire in me to be more than what I was or what others said. It may have lain dormant for years but it came from her. Daddy taught me to work hard regardless of what it is I'm doing. He also instilled in me to love what I do. Through the pair of them I'm a little of both.

The one thing I didn't get a lot of was physical affection. I knew my parents loved me but the words were never spoken. As children my sister and brothers and I didn't run to daddy for hugs and kisses. Nor did we get those things from mama. It wasn't until I was married and pregnant that I can recall ever kissing my daddy and giving him a hug. It is such vivid memories as these that even now give me goose bumps to think about it. As for mama it was even later than that. I had already been married twice and at one time I even had to move back home with her for a while. It was during this time at home again that mama battled breast cancer. It didn't have a chance! Her indomitable spirit had mama home after a couple of weeks and back at work after two more weeks. In between her going for her treatments and then heading to work mama still tried to put everybody else first. Mama was a strong woman, much stronger than I had ever given her credit for. It shouldn't have been a surprise of course after all I got it from her.

Now that I'm a parent and a grandparent I understand even more the importance of the role I play in my children's and grandchildren's lives. I give hugs and kisses and say I love you. I remember to offer words of encouragement and support especially during those times they may have made some unwise decisions and choices. Unconditional love is what mama taught me and I pray I'm passing it on to the next generations.

Through my life I am able to see how important the beginning is, but, it's not as important as the ending. This too I've learned through my own life. It's the reason for this book.

Chapter 2 – Influences of Friends

For as long as I can remember I had always been a pleaser. So much so that it was important to me to not ever have anyone upset or angry with me. That's all well and good but, if in the process you can no longer define whom you are except by others' opinions, then there's a major problem and it needs to be fixed. If not, you're destined to remain in the valley much longer than is needed. You see the choices we make have a domino effect that goes far beyond the immediate.

This made me think back to my high school years and the friends or lack thereof and how it molded me. There were two experiences that colored my perception of men and women for a very long time. Let me explain.

My first year of high school was an awkward time. My best friend from grade school attended the same high school but for a while we weren't together. I'll tell you more about her in a minute. I was smart, shy, clumsy, and skinny as a rail, no chest and just plain lonely. The only friends were those who wanted to copy off my test paper or needed help with other class assignments. As such I was starving to be a part of the in-crowd. So much so that one day a classmate invited me to her house to hang out after school and I accepted. Yes I did... I broke the rules my parents had set for me. And my disobedience caused me to be in a place I shouldn't have been.

My classmate and I went to her room and watched TV and talked. I was truly enjoying myself. At one point my classmate asked if I wanted something to drink and I said sure. She left to get us some kool-aid and something to snack on. While she was gone I just relaxed on the bed. I jumped when the door opened thinking I'd need to give her a hand. Instead in walked her brother and two of his friends. I was 13, and before I could understand totally the ramifications of what was happening I found myself being held down and raped. Even now, thirty-eight years later I am not able to tell you how I made it out of the house.

All I remember was the pain between my legs and the feeling of something sticky running down my legs. I managed to walk/run more than 2 miles home. Once there I quickly went to the bathroom, wiped my tears, washed up and threw away the clothes I'd been wearing. I then proceeded to prepare dinner for my 3 brothers and my sister and help them with homework.

When daddy got home I fixed his plate, and when mama came home that night I had her special shake ready and waiting for her. I never opened my mouth. At school I buried my head in books and shied even more from people. The girl, her brother and his two friends avoided me like the plague. I realized years later that perhaps they were waiting for the police to come or some other action to be taken.

When I share this experience with other women, one of the first questions I'm asked is, "Why didn't you tell"? My answer: it was my fault. I asked for it because I disobeyed my parents' rules therefore it was my punishment. I no longer believe that but that's where a 13 year olds' logic stood.

That experience not only resulted in the loss of my virginity in such a violent manner but it also caused me to mistrust anyone I didn't already know. My guard was always up. I waited to see when the disappointment would come or I simply remained a loner, never trusting myself to trust too many people.

But there was one friendship forged long before that incident, which left a glimmer of hope for real friends remain alive in me. According to the dictionary, the definitions of the word Friend are as follows: a favored companion, one that is not hostile, one attached to another by affection or esteem or an acquaintance. My personal definition of a friend is a rare and precious jewel one to be cherished and nurtured.

There are all kinds of friends; the degree of importance you place on these friends and the type of friend you are in turn, determines the depth and longevity of that friendship. Think about it, the first friends you ever had were most likely made when you were in grade school. You met them either in the classroom, on the school bus or on the playground at recess.

In grade school my best friend and I were very close. We became friends when the school bully tried to take my lunch money, and she came to my rescue. After that we always rode the school bus together and sat whispering secrets all the way to school.

We sat near each other in class, we even got caught a few times passing notes when we should have been listening to the teacher. We always sat at the same old table at lunchtime and managed to dislike the same foods; we even played together at recess. We were together so much, that the school bully knew better than to bother us when he saw us. Do you have a memory of that first friend in grade school?

In high school my friend and I would walk to school together every day. We usually shared the same circle of friends, but once, for a while, we seemed to grow apart. It was during that time apart that the previous incident occurred.

We found our way back and vowed never to let that happen again. Together we tried out for the cheerleading squad, I didn't make it but I was happy for my friend and helped her learn her cheers. We talked for hours on the phone about everything and nothing. Thank God we never liked the same boy! Our friendship was much more important than any boy could ever be. We swapped clothes and for a short time we even dressed alike. My friend even taught me how to do my hair so I could have an Afro like everyone else. We were together so much that people thought of the two of us as twins; if you saw one you saw the other.

When we were 16 we went on our first movie date together, although we didn't see much of the movie. We saw the Exorcist and had our hands over our faces through the majority of the movie. We cried together over sentimental movies and laughed at each other's lame jokes. We were more like sisters instead of friends. We lost touch when she went off to college. Amazingly, when I began to work in my purpose and mission she was one of the first to answer the call to join the cause.

I made very few new friends but I did have acquaintances with which I discussed serious issues like world poverty and world peace. My new friends introduced me to some new experiences, some good, others not so good. One thing they introduced to me was alcohol. Of course alcohol didn't agree with me and so my friends stayed with me and held cold towels to my head while I had an intimate conversation with Mr. Toilet. These friendships never lasted long. But I always remembered my best friend that I'd gone to grade school and high school with. One day I just had to pick up the phone and call just to say hello! It was like we'd never been apart. The years fell away and there we were friends and sisters rolled into one.

Whenever I speak to young girls I always share my high school experience. Not just the experience but also the lessons I learned from them. I have to because too many times I've had them tell me that they give in to peer-pressure because they don't want to be isolated or ostracized. I let them know that they are not alone and that many have faced these same challenges. I then share with them the lessons I took from the experience. I believe it gives them hope. I pray it can do the same for you.

I've learned that all through life we meet people and by the time we are responsible adults, the time we have to spend with friends becomes limited; and so the need to put a degree of importance to them becomes necessary. There are the friends you have at work, whom for the most part you don't have any associations with outside of work. There can be those rare occasions when the friendship does spill outside of work, but that's the exception. Then you have your Friday and Saturday night friends that you go to the clubs and party with. But if you're married or have outgrown that stage, then you're probably content to have a small get together with a few intimate friends for a few hours at your house or theirs. Then there's the friend you discus your spiritual beliefs and pray with. There's the friend you can call in the middle of the night and they'll come just to hold your hand. There's the friend that as you were growing up she was called Mom, now she's mom and friend. There's the friend that knows when to give advice and when to just listen.

It's up to you to determine what type of friends you have and what type of friend you are. My early experiences with friendship stayed with me for many years. To let go of the ghosts from my past was not easy.

It hurt so deep, which meant, I was still in the valley holding on and not opening up to something better.

It's never easy but I promise if you've experienced anything like I've described, I implore you, release it, the best is yet to come.

Today, my husband is my best friend and I feel blessed to have at least 2 or 3 more people in my life that I can call true friends. As a matter of fact in the last 4 years my sister-in law Betty, who's married to my brother, Ronnie, has crossed from just being a sister-in-law, she's my sister and my friend.

I believe that true friends are a rarity. True friendship requires work. It doesn't happen over night; it must be nurtured with love, kindness and respect. 'A true friend is one who reaches for your hand and touches your heart.' In my life my heart is full.

Phase II – Releasing the Junk

Chapter 3 – Letting Go of Marriage Woes

Release: To set free from restraint, confinement, or servitude, to let go. To relieve from something that confine, burdens, or oppresses, to give up in favor of another.

Junk: Secondhand, worn, or discarded articles; something of poor quality; something of little meaning, worth, or significance

Releasing the junk I equate to cleaning out your closet. Ladies, you know how we are. Go take a look in your closet right now...go on I'll wait. Now, be honest of all the dresses, suits, pants, sweaters, and coats and other accessories (not counting the shoes) do you actually wear? If you're like me you have a couple of favorite pair of shoes, and the others... well they caught your eye and you just can't bear to part with them. Or, what about that suit back in the corner? I know you paid good money for it, even caught it on sale, but that was at least 2 sizes ago. So why can't you part with it? Sentimental you say....

What value does it bring to your life? Or, is it taking up space that could be used for something more positive and fulfilling? Cleaning out your closet may take you some time but the benefits far outweigh the effort required.

I've found a system to make it a little easier for me; perhaps it could be useful for you too. Not too long ago a shelf broke in my closet and my husband informed me that he'd fix it as soon as I took things out of the closet so he could have easy access.

Sounded like the perfect time to do some spring-cleaning. Of course I wanted to wait until he would be out of the house for a while. I had some serious business to take care of and I wanted no distractions.

When the opportunity presented itself I took everything out of the closet, creating separate piles on the bedroom floor. Shoes in one pile, dresses in another and so on. Then I stripped to my bra and panties... don't worry there's a purpose for this. For each item on the bedroom floor I asked myself the following questions.

1. Can I still wear it?

2. Am I comfortable?

3. Is it outdated?

4. When was the last time I wore it?

5. When will I wear it again?

Some I had to try on, thus the stripping to my bra and panties (quite a few I couldn't get in). From there I started 3 new sections. Keep, Goodwill and Junk. The process took me more than 3 hours. I'd hate to think how long it would have taken if I had a larger closet. Suffice it to say, my husband was pleased for all of 30 seconds. You see now I had to go shopping. Interestingly enough this exercise gave me the idea for this book .So if you're not busy I want to invite you to come along as I share my insights.

So what Junk did I need to release? It wasn't difficult to figure out. All I needed to do was to start with my high school years and then move on to my failed marriages.

I have never attended a single high school reunion. Why, because for a long time I did not want to run into the girl, her brother or his friends. Logic did not reside in my mind to say perhaps they weren't even there. Nor did it dawn on me that perhaps they might have forgotten about the incident. Either way I didn't want to take the chance. These thoughts and feelings let me know I was still holding on to the hurt, pain and betrayal. I knew I'd moved past it when my choice to not attend had nothing to with them, but my acknowledging that I did not need apologies from them to be whole. I still don't attend simply because I don't want to.

Then there are my failed marriages. The first was before even graduating high school. This marriage came about because I got pregnant and being old-fashioned my daddy told my boyfriend he was going to make an honest woman out of me. Honest, woman! Whoa! We're going a little too fast here. But in October 1974 my parents went to the courthouse and signed the papers for me to get married.

Suddenly I was thrust into the role of wife and expectant mother and still in high school! Talk about pressure and fear! Looking back on that time neither of us were emotionally mature enough to be married let alone parents. At the time I was 17 and he was 22. Adjusting to each other was not an easy chore.

When I was 3 months pregnant I had to visit the local health department. Why? Because my husband had been intimate with another woman (girl) and contracted a venereal disease. Imagine the hurt and pain I felt, not to mention the affect I feared it could pose to my unborn child. I prayed hard that he would be fine. It seemed that we were always arguing about something or blaming the other. When I was 6 months pregnant our arguing resulted in me falling down a flight of stairs outside our apartment. Fortunately, God saw fit to allow me to bring forth my first born with no physical or emotional problems. After David was born we tried to settle down and be a family. A year and a half later my second son Dion was born.

David and Dion were and are to this day my pride and joy. Of course babies cannot fix a marriage and so by the time the boys were 4 and 5 years old we had separated. Two years later we were divorced. My second marriage wasn't much better. You'd think I would have learned a few things by then. I tell people that I spent a lot of time in the valley so I could share with others how not to stay there. It doesn't mean that they will heed the advice but at least the information has been shared.

When I met my second husband I was struggling to hold things together. I'd lost my job at the hospital and could only find very minimal work. This meant I depended on Family and Children Services to keep my household together. Don't get me wrong the assistance was needed and appreciated but I couldn't wait to not have strangers judging me. It made me feel inadequate or like I was begging someone else to take care of my responsibilities. Right around that time I met the person that would become my second husband. Already the circumstances were a recipe for disaster.

My second marriage had two very needy people. I needed help to keep my household together and he just needed a household. Sure he said all the things I wanted to hear and for the first couple of years we were pretty happy. Then things began to change. I couldn't go anywhere without his permission, not even to visit my mom. Many times he would have called my mom's house a couple of times before I made it there. Slowly, without warning I found myself seeing my family less and less.

I had become isolated and only associated with his friends. When the arguing turned to physical attacks I knew I was going to have to make a change. But I was afraid of what he might do and how I'd make it. The day I discovered he'd stolen my Rich's (Now Macy's) Department Store card and shopped for his girlfriend erased any lingering doubts I may have harbored about my intentions to leave. One I day waited until he'd gone to work and I packed the boys clothes to send them to spend the weekend with their dad. He didn't pick them up often but this time was perfect because I could make my escape.

That night my husband returned home to a half empty apartment but he knew where I worked so he came storming up there. This was back in the early 80's so my knowledge of how to handle things through the courts was next to nil. He stalked me at my job and at my new apartment for weeks. Once he even forced his way into the apartment and when I tried to call the police he ripped the phone out of the wall. I was so scared!!

Just for a moment I considered getting back with him just to keep the peace. But when I looked into the eyes of my boys I knew I had to be strong and not give in. For safety purposes one of my brothers moved in with me. Eventually my husband moved out of state and a couple of years later I received my divorce and took back my maiden name.

It is only now that I can acknowledge that each marriage had some form of domestic violence. I've learned that a successful marriage is one in which neither party needs the other but have respect and love for each other and want to be together. This was reaffirmed when I married my current husband, Oscar. As I've gone to different places and shared my story I've seen the old me in many of the women in attendance. This continues to be conformation that I am working in the purpose and mission God gave me.

Therefore, I refuse to be ashamed of any part of my life. Each experience has provided a nugget of truth that when explored reveals value about me and the world around me. It is for this reason that I want to encourage you to begin the process of clearing the junk in your life. You don't have to do it all at once. The project may be too big, so break it up into manageable tasks. I suggest starting with how you see yourself; then how others see you. There is a correlation between the two and I remember making my own list after my second marriage failed.

My list had two columns, one listed what I thought about myself and the other listed what others thought. This is what it looked like:

ME	OTHERS
Stupid	Stupid
Needy	Needy
Ugly	Ugly
Skinny	Skinny
4-eyes	4-eyes
Bad hair	Nappy Head
Timid	Pushover
Self-Concious	Easy
Smart	Brainy

Once I looked at this list I was horrified. It seems that what I thought about myself depended solely on what others thought about me. No wonder I had very low self-esteem! Now the challenge would be to make a change. This was extremely important to me. I had two young sons I had to raise and I wanted to give them the very best of me. But first, I had to find it.

Chapter 4 – Single Parenthood

In 1986 and I was a single parent raising two very boisterous and all-male sons. At the time they were 9 and 10 years old, perfect age for trouble, and I do mean TROUBLE. I had recently been hired by a fast food chain as an assistant manager. The pay was good but the hours long and hard. This meant that for the most part my boys came home from school with just enough time for me to give them instructions. You know the kind.

· No one in the house

· Eat your dinner

· Do your homework

· Don't go outside

· In the bed by 8:00pm

Right...rarely happened. I had to do a lot of raising them via the telephone to keep them in check. As the saying goes, out of sight out of mind and it definitely applied to those two. Many times I called and didn't get an answer and had to call a neighbor to check on them for me (this was back in the day when neighbors looked out for each other whenever possible). Returning home I was always grateful to see the house still standing and my two angels sleeping peacefully in their beds.

I hated leaving them alone so much but I felt I had no other choice. It was my responsibility to take care of and provide for them as well as myself. I remember many nights crying and wishing I had help. It was a heartfelt desire, yet not one I actually believed would happen. You see my history with men was nothing to brag about.

And so it was that one evening at work, after making my usual phone call I laid my head on my desk in the office. The door to the office opened and this deep Voice asked, "Are you all right?" To this day I don't remember looking up, only softly responding that I was okay. The company I worked for hired security for the evenings, not just for the restaurant but also as an escort at the close of the evening when the managers had to make a night deposit at the bank. Only petty cash was left in the restaurant overnight. That particular day I have to admit I was feeling sorry for myself. I'd had a lot of practice beating myself up because of my lot in life. In many ways I thought I was the dumbest person on the face of the earth. Yes, I can admit this now. But I've come a long ways since then.

The voice quickly left the office to take up his post in the lobby. I made one final call home and said good night to the boys. Since this was the middle of the week and it was a slow night, I spent a lot of my time in the office. Suddenly there was a loud commotion coming from the front line, which required my attention.

On my way to investigate I checked on the cook to make sure he wasn't cooking more product than was needed. Just as I came around the corner I saw my two cashiers and the biscuit maker surrounding the voice. I quickly assessed the situation and saw that the voice held a dime that each of the girls claimed belonged to her.

Okay ladies let's get real. The object of their desire was not the dime, but the person holding the dime. Well, I needed my employees to get back to work so I walked into the middle of this little circle and stuck out my hand. The voice placed the dime in my hand and just like that my employees went back to their stations.

"Can I talk to you?" the voice asked. It was only then did I notice the man to whom the voice belonged. And I very emphatically responded, "NO". I proceeded to do my register check and yes, let's be honest I stole more than one or two glances at the man behind the voice. As discreetly as possible, I was able to determine that he was about my height (maybe a little shorter...), milk chocolate complexion and two of the most gorgeous dimples I'd ever seen on a man. Well, I do have very good powers of observation! It was going to be a very long night. At one point in the evening I needed to go across the street to the little convenience store to see if I could get $5.00 worth of pennies to make it through closing and the voice accompanied me there.

Again he asked, "Can I talk to you?" I smiled and again responded with not as much conviction as before a soft 'No'. Well to make a long story short at the end of the night my ride (one of the cashiers) suddenly had other plans and I found myself relying on the voice to get me safely home.

It has been many years since that night, more than twenty-two to be exact. And the owner of the voice has been seeing me safely home ever since. I didn't realize at the time the significance of that night. It turned out to be the first step on my journey to a fresh start. But first God and I had some work to do.

Chapter 5 – Spiritual Connection

It was also during this time that I began to crave a closer relationship with God but had no clue how to accomplish that. Since I was 6 or 7 years old I'd always gone to church. I attended Sunday school and was even baptized in the well in front of the little country church but it didn't really resonate with me.

It was near the end of my second marriage that my boys and I began to attend church on a regular basis. A big part of it was because there I had peace and the boys could associate with other children.

The other part was I just wanted companionship that did not cause me pain. I began to have a glimmer of hope that my life could be changed for the better and I wanted it. It seems the harder things got in my second marriage the more I sought God.

One day after a very trying day at work and other issues that I had faced I took pen and paper and had a conversation with God. I know to some this may sound strange but believe me this is exactly what happened.

On the day in question I'd had more than a few challenges and felt the need to express the gratitude I felt for God and His Son. So I grabbed paper and pen and this is what I wrote.

My Conversation

Hello…. May I speak to God? Hello God, it's me. Oh, you know.

Well, I wanted to know if I could have a few minutes of your time. All the time I need. Really! Thank-you!

I don't usually call on you, but I've been going through some things lately and I need your advice… You've been waiting for me! But, how... never mind I know you're everywhere.

You see God, it's like this, I don't have any friends, except those that want something from me. And that makes me sad.

You'll be my friend! So, what do you want? It can't be much I don't have anything worth much.

Just Me! But, what can you do with me? Yes, I know, you created the earth in 6 days and then you made Man. Yes, I remember, from the dust. I guess you're saying that if you could do all that then that's nothing compared to what you can do with me.

How did I sleep last night? Well, I was so tired that I fell asleep as soon as my head hit the pillow. The next thing I knew the sun's shining through my window and when I looked at the clock it was time to get up.

You did! Just for me! Why thank you God! That was the nicest, quietest alarm I've ever had. I lay in the bed for a few minutes worrying about the bills, and wondering how I was going to feed the children.

I got up, took my shower, got dressed and went and woke up the boys. There was just enough oatmeal for the 2 of them, but it was such a beautiful day, that I thought I'd take them to the park. We were on our way out the door when my brother stopped by. I hadn't seen him in quite a while. He decided to join us at the park and later when the boys said they were hungry, he bought them both a Happy Meal.

After eating we went back home and I sent the boys to take a nap. My brother and I sat and talked for a while, and then he said he had to go, so I walked him to the door. After he left I found 5 twenty-dollar bills on the counter. All I could do was cry.

You whispered in his ear! Thank-you God!

I walked to the grocery store with the boys. I bought juice and eggs and milk and so much more. Actually it was my lucky day. They were having a buy 1 get 1 free sale and just about everything on sale I bought. I managed to buy so many groceries that it was much more than the 3 of us could carry home. I was wondering what to do when a neighbor stopped and offered us a ride.

Don't tell me, that was you!

When we got back there was a note on the door. I had 10 days to pay the rent. I just sighed and laid it on the table. I wanted to scream out my frustrations, but I knew that wouldn't do any good. And besides I didn't want to upset the boys.

I sent my oldest to the mailbox. You wouldn't believe what he brought back. There stuck among all the bills was a letter from my old job. It said they were holding a check in my name, and when I read the amount I was speechless. It was enough to pay the rent AND the utilities. I knew then that it was my day of miracles.

After the boys took their baths and went to bed, I picked up my old Bible, the one I haven't read in such a long time. I didn't know where to start, so I went to the 23 Psalms. And that's when I knew I needed to talk to you.

I want to thank-you, God for being there even when I've lost all hope. Thank You for Your Love and Your Mercy and Your Grace. But most of all thank you for your Son. For I know he shed his blood for a sinner like me.

I was wondering, when you talk to him. Will you give Him a message? Tell Him that I Love Him. Would you tell Him that and that…?

What! Tell him myself! You can't be serious… Yes! Okay… Hello, Jesus…

Chapter 6 – Secrets & Mercy

In 1987 I attended the funeral of the grandmother of a close friend of mine. It was the first such occasion that I had attended as a young adult and it had a profound effect on me. The family was from a small country town in South Georgia and so everyone knew everyone else. There was no such thing as secrets in that town, or so it was thought. My friend, Renee* had not seen her grandmother in a few months.

She explained to me once that there were things that she and her grandmother could not come to terms with and so she moved to the city to get away. Not only that, but she and her siblings did not have a close relationship. So when she asked me to accompany her, I agreed. It was a rainy dreary morning, with no sign that the sun would manage to peek through the clouds. We drove in silence except for the sound of the radio and after a while we even turned that off. I peeked over at my friend several times on the 2- hour drive but I could tell that she was deep in thought. I silently said a prayer that she and the rest of the family would get through the day and find some peace and solace in the company of each other.

As we drove into the church's parking lot I noticed that there were only 3 other cars there. So I parked next to the red mustang and waited on my friend. She took a deep breath and made a long sigh before opening the car door. I noticed that she stood erect with her head held high and went into the church. Not wanting to intrude on such a solemn occasion I followed discreetly behind her.

As we entered the church I saw 2 young men whom I took to be her brothers and another young woman who I assumed was her sister. I sat down in the back of the church and watched as my friend slowly made her way to the rest of the family. There was an awkward silence at first and then I heard one of her brothers speak.

"Well, look who has decided to grace us with her presence." Her sister punched him gently on the arm and admonished him, "be nice, this is neither the time nor the place for your attitude." I noticed a slight smile cross my friend's face but then just as suddenly it disappeared. I heard her sister say, "Well what have you to say for yourself? I believe you owe us all an apology! After all you're the reason grandma is dead, it broke her heart when you moved away. How could you be so selfish?"

My friend looked as if someone had punched her in the stomach. She slowly turned around and started walking back the way she'd come. I wanted to go to her and put my arms around her but, it was as if there was this invisible hand that kept me rooted in place. Once the feeling left me though I went out of the church to look for her but she was nowhere to be found. I went back inside and could hear her brothers and sister arguing. I so wanted to tell them that life was too short to not have a close relationship with your family but I could tell it would fall on deaf ears.

In the middle of the bickering a policeman came into the church and asked if this was the funeral for a Mrs. Mamie Brown*? The older of the young men acknowledged that it was and asked the officer what was the problem. I heard the policeman explain that he had run across a young woman who was walking along the highway and crying. He managed to get her name and discovered that she was here to attend her grandmother's funeral. So he brought her to the church but he was having difficulty getting her to come inside.

During all of this I could sense the impatience that permeated from the other siblings but the younger brother looked at the officer and asked, "Is she in any kind of trouble?"

"No," the officer replied.

"Well could you please ask her to come inside?" I heard the younger brother ask. The officer said he'd give it another try, but before he turned to go outside I saw him hand what looked like a letter to the older brother.

He explained that he saw her drop it when he stopped to help. No one it seems had noticed me and so I felt trapped. There I was witnessing private matters yet unable to leave my spot. Everyone crowded around the older sibling as he began to read the letter the officer had given him.

Even now I can hear him reading it … this is what it said.

My darling Renee,*

I've been holding this in for such a long time and I'm tired. I pray it's not too late to ask for your forgiveness. I know growing up without your parents was hard and now after all you've been through I wish I could go back and do things differently. When your aunt offered to raise you with your cousins I said no. How could I know I was sentencing you to such trauma?

After Grandpa Henry* died and I later married Grandpa Dan I thought everything would be all right. With you and Grandpa Dan* I thought I could handle my grief over losing your mother. You were such a happy child at first; even though you were young you had love for everyone.

When you were born I know you were a shock to your brothers and sisters and so they didn't get to know the sweet child you were. I'm only sorry that circumstances conspired to kill that love and joy you possessed.

I'm even sorrier that I didn't listen when you tried to tell me what was going on. I didn't want to believe it I guess but now I have the proof. You see I was up cleaning the attic last night trying to get things organized when I ran across a shoe box full of pictures.

I wondered why they were up there and not in the albums downstairs, so I opened it to get a closer look. Oh, my sweet baby! Those indecent and awful pictures showing you in poses too old for such a child and the look of sadness and pleading in your eyes just broke my heart! I screamed and cursed the day I ever married that man. Oh honey! Please, forgive me! I understand now what you had been trying to tell me. No wonder you felt alone and betrayed!

But baby, please give your brothers and sister a chance to help you. They'll be there for you, much more so than I ever was. I burned the pictures and you'll never have to see them again. I got rid of anything that reminded me of that man and the pain he caused you. It's going to be a long road to healing but I know with God anything is possible. And I pray that one day you can forgive an old fool for not listening and being there when you needed me most. Lean on your family and give them a chance to prove to you that you can trust and depend on them. Let them show you that you don't have to walk this path alone.

    All my love, Grandma

*Names have been changed to protect privacy

When I heard him stop reading I noticed that there were tears in everyone's eyes including mine. And then the policeman was there, bringing Renee* back into the church. Everyone was hugging and kissing her and asking for her forgiveness.

It was about that time that the sun broke through the clouds and bathed the church in beautiful light. And, as if on cue, the other mourners began to enter the church. I never mentioned what I had witnessed to my friend but I never forgot.

In my heart I believe that I had witnessed God's Mercy at work mending a broken family. The experience encouraged me to try again to get my own family closer together. We did manage to make a little headway but not as much as I would have liked. But for many years we did spend more time with each other and our extended families.

These two incidents gave me the encouragement I needed to continue on the road to letting go. Ever so slowly I began to pay a little closer attention at church to what the pastor was saying. Sometimes I felt like he was talking just to me but at others nothing he said made any sense. There were times I wanted to talk to him and ask questions. I even made an appointment to see him one day but the conversation left me feeling empty and unfulfilled. I tried picking up the bible and reading it to find the truths within. Slowly, ever so slowly a light began to appear.

Within the pages of the Bible I began to see a different me, one that was loved by God and his Son. I saw qualities that before, I never knew I had. I made a list that described not only the person I wanted to be and was but also the type of people that belonged in my circle. I had a new list and it was good.

Love

Beautiful

Joy

Honest

Loyal

Hardworking

Generous

Now I'm getting somewhere! If God sees these things in me then I must be worthwhile. I have something to offer. I don't have to answer to the old words. They don't belong. I had to start believing it and practicing it. So every morning I'd look in the mirror and repeat those words to myself. I would say them with conviction and power. The more I said them the more I began to believe them.

It wasn't instantaneous, it took work and along the way I had a few setbacks. But I persevered. I had a purpose. I needed to show my children a better way. My boys had witnessed some of my struggles and my desire for them was that they'd not follow the examples before them. It's not easy raising boys. Mothers, we do a good job but there are some things that only a man can teach them. But the things we do teach them we must do well. My boys were a handful and I'm sure even now there are things they got away with that I don't know about; especially when I was working those long hours at the restaurant. So many times I recall the excitement they had whenever their father promised to pick them up for the weekend. And I've witnessed their pain and disappointment as they sat on the stoop waiting for a car to pick them up that never arrived. I saw the sadness in their eyes when their friends played with their fathers and the longing in their eyes to do the same. It took all the strength I had to not berate their father in front of them, but I had always promised myself I'd be the bigger person.

I needed my boys to know without a doubt that they were loved. And so I was careful to not invite men to my home until I got to know them better. The boys did not need to see me with a different man every few weeks or months. I owed them stability.

It is for this reason that I had rules I needed to abide by. Those rules included the following:

· Accept that the children are not separate but inclusive in the relationship – your children are your first priority. They deserve stability as much as possible. Children are like sponges and soak up whatever is in their environment.

· Never sacrifice quality time with your children for the opportunity to date. On those occasions when you are dating reassure your children that you're coming back and nothing is changing. They deserve to have their feelings accounted for.

· Allow yourself ample time to get to know a person before inviting them to meet your children. There's no rush. Be content with where you are.

· Be realistic in your expectations; realize that just because you like the new guy it does not automatically mean the same will be true for the children.

These rules served me well when I met Oscar. It was several weeks before I introduced him to the boys. Even though Oscar and I spent time together I made sure that my boys always knew that they were not forgotten. I didn't just jump into a new relationship and assume that things would be fine with them. I had to protect them, which meant their needs came before mine. They were the innocent ones. When I finally did introduce him to the boys it was instant dislike on the boys' part. It was years later that they admitted they could tell he was going to be trouble for them.

Chapter 7 - Forgiveness

The final step in releasing the junk in my life would require all the strength and courage I could muster. It was also in this step that my then friend, Oscar played a role. UNFORGIVENESS can wreak havoc in a person's life. It prevents you from taking chances or trusting. It can also make you HATE if you're not careful. In the past I tended to be very closed-mouth and kept all my feelings to myself. As a result I could look in my little address book and maybe find 10 names inside and half of those were family. As much as I wanted a different life I had absolutely no clue how to attain it.

This final breakthrough caught me totally by surprise. Oscar had come over after work. After the boys had completed their homework, taken baths and gone to bed we sat watching television. The show was In the Heat of the Night and this particular episode dealt with a woman who had been violently raped but no one believed her. That night I got extremely agitated and I found myself screaming at the show and the actors. Suddenly the floodgates opened and I started bawling like a baby. I felt Oscar grab my hand and before I could stop myself it all came out. The molestation when I was about 8 or 9, the rape at 13, two failed marriages and even the night I was kidnapped from a phone booth and taken far away and raped and left to fend for myself.

The anger came flowing out that I had kept pent up inside; because it seemed everyone depended on me but there was no one who came to my aid. I was angry because no matter how hard I tried I couldn't develop a close relationship with my sister or any of my brothers like I wanted. And I was especially angry with myself for being so weak and needy. Through it all Oscar just gently rubbed my back while I cried until there were no more tears to cry.

Exhausted I slumped back on the sofa and it was then that Oscar began to share with me that it was time for me to forgive. Forgive, such a little word but oh so powerful. He explained that I needed to not only forgive the people I felt had wronged me but that I needed to forgive myself as well. Forgiving others I could do. But forgiving me, well, that's a different thing entirely.

I remember him saying, "With God you can." And with that he took me by the hand and walked me to the bathroom. Once there he made me look in the mirror, "Tell me what you see", he said. And I responded, "I see wild hair, red eyes and a runny nose." It's true, I think had the boys been awake I would have scared them to death.

"You know what I see?" he asked. I shook my head. "I see a woman full of love, who first needs to love herself". And then we had bible study. Through the night he talked with me, listened to me and encouraged me.

I finally forgave my boys' father for betraying me when I was pregnant with my first child. I even forgave the classmate, her brother and his friends. They were old baggage I needed to let go of. Surely after all these years I was no longer in their memory banks so why should they be in mine. It took me a little longer to forgive my second husband. This is because I blamed him for my not having closure when the police were able to arrest suspects in my kidnapping and rape. He wouldn't allow me to go to the police station and take a look at a lineup. He said I needed to forget about it and move on. At the time I didn't have the backbone to go against what he said. And so I was always left with a feeling of disappointment, regret and unfinished business.

I forgave my brothers and sister for always depending on me but not being there when I needed help. Even though I stopped asking and therefore never gave them a chance to do anything different. I forgave mama for making me take on more responsibility than I was ready for. I forgave myself for being weak and needing approval. I looked at the world around me and realized it wasn't such a bad place. Bad things had happened to me but it didn't make me bad. To make that distinction was true growth.

By the time I laid my head down to sleep I felt as if I'd been hit by a Mack truck. I slept and slept. I don't know for how long, but I do remember the feeling I had upon waking. It was euphoria, peace and something much more important. I felt free.

My junk was gone, now on to the business of living. Don't get me wrong this was by no means an easy process. And there were setbacks along the way. But because I truly desired something better, not only for my children, but for me as well. I was determined to see it through. Anything worth having requires sacrifice and work. If you're ready and willing to do the work then the reward will be invaluable. All I have to say is: Go for it!

Phase III – Revealing the Jewels

Chapter 8 – A Blended Family

Now that the final piece of junk had been released I was ready to reveal the jewels that were present in my life. The very first jewel was my family. My immediate family, the ones I saw on a daily basis. This family consisted of my sons, my new husband, Oscar and me.

We're a blended family, the label society gives us is stepfamily. I can attest to the fact that blended or stepfamilies have their own unique set of issues; but it does not have to depict the negative that society tends to thrust upon us. Funny, we laugh about it now because it was a love/hate relationship on the part of the boys. Let me tell you a little about them and how they got along with the new person in my life.

Once I made up my mind that I was willing to give this person a chance, I decided to introduce Oscar to the two most important people in my life. Right away I could see their guard up and I noticed that the boys paid close attention to how he spoke to me. I think they wanted to see if he'd raise his voice or worse his hand to me. Don't get me wrong they were polite, but cautious.

They also tested him as well. I'll never forget the day my oldest David, took Oscar's radio apart, he'd tried to put it back together but he had pieces left over. I just knew he'd pushed the final straw. Instead Oscar sat him down and they had a man-to-man conversation. He explained to David that it was important to respect other people's property and that what he'd done was wrong. In the end David apologized and although Oscar accepted the apology I could tell he was still a bit angry. He earned a few brownie points in my book because he remained the adult.

Now Dion, well he was a different story altogether. He could be the sweetest child but you better watch out! I'll never forget the day I was at work and he called and asked what I wanted for dinner. If I hadn't mentioned it before I taught both boys to cook at a very early age. This skill has served them well over the years. Both are good cooks and have even taught their wives a thing or two.

Anyway here's my son planning to surprise me for dinner, the thought put a smile on my face. It lasted all of 45 minutes. The next phone call I received was from the grocery store. It seems Dion had gone shopping, for the food he planned to prepare for dinner. Only he didn't have any money. Here I was stuck at work, no ride and frantic. I tried to call the boy's father to no avail. Finally I called Oscar and without hesitation he went to talk to the store manager.

Of course he did more than just pick him up. We had a mutual friend who was a member of the Atlanta Police Department, whom Oscar called for a favor. He wanted to teach Dion a lesson about where stealing could land him. He called me to tell me his plan. I wasn't keen on the idea but I had begun to trust his instincts. So for about 45 minutes Dion spent time in juvenile detention. Oscar said he walked in bad and bold, but near the end he started to cry. They brought him out and the officer talked to him about what he'd done. It would be nice to say that he'd learned his lesson. He was 9 and I wasn't that lucky. Naturally Oscar was now definitely enemy #1 with both the boys. I think the two of them started plotting their revenge right then and there!

I'll never forget that night I came home from work and the house was dark. Not one light was on. When I got inside the boys were nowhere to be found. Lying in the middle of the floor was Oscar's brand new silk shirt he'd just bought that day and left at the house. It was covered in black shoe polish. I panicked! I started calling the neighbors and their friends. Oscar just stood there with this look of utter disbelief, holding what remained of his silk shirt. I called mama, my brothers, everybody I could think of with no results. It was the last number I called that calmed my nerves. The boys were at their father's house. It was the next day when I learned that after they realized just how much trouble they could be in that they decided to run away. Thank God their father's house was as far as they got. It was a couple of weeks after this before I would see Oscar again. Part of me figured he'd had enough. As it turns out he was dealing with an issue regarding his own children.

In the midst of us getting to know each other Oscar brought his kids to meet the boys. I must admit I was surprised to see how well they got along. Whenever he could he'd bring them around so they could spend time together and get to know each other. When Oscar's children's mom decided to move the family to New Orleans, which he'd only found out by accident, it left him little time to try and make other arrangements for the children. The night their mom drove them to New Orleans he managed to make it there with just enough time to hug his children and tell them that he loved them. Of course at the time he still had no idea exactly where in New Orleans they were moving to. I'll never forget the look on his face when he showed up at my door. Until then I had never seen a grown man cry. It just broke my heart. It was then that I told him that he could lavish all of his love and caring on my two boys. It wasn't easy for any of them, but I watched and marveled as they all began to interact with each other. Heck, they even had "Just the Boys" excursions. Oscar worked hard to gain their trust and in turn earned their respect.

There was one thing that my boys and I were not use to and that was having someone with strong opinions. Let me be clear, I do love my husband, but there were times before we were married and even now that I just don't like him. He could be very critical sometimes to the point of hurting ones feelings. Many times he made us feel as if we were always in the wrong. I've learned since then that in many ways I was still dealing with my insecurity regarding my own self-worth. Once I regained my confidence I was able to stop reading negatives from him and instead received the encouragement he offered. Still I say he's stubborn and at times likes to be in total control.

Through the years we each have had demons we needed to vanquish before we could solidify our union. I had two failed marriages, he had one and with them baggage that needed to be discarded. It took quite a long time for us both to reach the stage where we knew we were ready to take that plunge again. When it happened I knew the old me was gone and in its place was the type of woman that could make a husband proud. I also knew that Oscar's baggage was no longer a factor and that he would make a wife (me) proud. And to top it all off my sons, gave their blessings, even throwing him a bachelor party!!

Our family blended into a whole new family December 9, 2000. When I see the relationship that has developed between my husband and my sons I am always filled with both pride and joy. Before marriage he was always addressed as Mr. Oscar, now he's just PaPa. The negative image of the word stepfamily doesn't live in our home. The proof, in our house we're just family. And this is my first jewel!

Chapter 9 - Courage

Before releasing my junk I rarely experienced new things, because I was bound by fear and mistrust. Once it was gone I was ready and willing to experience new things. One of my fondest experiences was my first airplane ride. My husband surprised me one year with a trip to Las Vegas. I have always been a little nervous about being in high places, so the idea of getting on an airplane left me with a stomach full of butterflies.

The entire week leading up to the trip I kept asking him questions. Will I be able to see outside the plane? What does it feel like when the plane takes off? Were you scared the first time you flew? Those were just a few of the questions I had and I must admit I asked them more than once. When the day arrived for us to leave, I awoke with a feeling of both dread and excitement. The closer we got to the airport and I could see what I was about to travel on, I began to have second thoughts. But not wanting to wimp out, I put on my brave face and followed my husband. Getting on the plane was easy, much easier then than now, in wake of the 911 tragedies.

We found our seats, which, we were informed were pretty good seats considering they were just a row back from being in first class. There wasn't a lot of move around room, so I just watched people getting on and wrestling to put their carry-on baggage in the overhead compartment; all the while working to keep the butterflies at bay. Oscar tried to engage me in conversation to keep me from thinking about this huge piece of metal that I was about to travel in. Eventually all the passengers were aboard and then the flight attendants started to explain some safety precautions. I don't remember it all, but I do know I looked around to see how far we were from the emergency exits.

When the airplane took off, the butterflies that had been asleep woke up. I held my husband's hand and closed my eyes. He managed to coax me into opening my eyes and to relax. I could feel the plane rolling down the runway and then suddenly I wasn't sitting so erect and I could feel the plane lift off. I have to admit I had the silliest grin on my face. Don't ask me to tell you what I was thinking; most likely I was just saying a prayer. After a while the light came on that let us know we could undo our seat belts and move around if we wanted. I really wasn't too interested in doing that at first. Once we'd been flying for a while the attendants started to serve breakfast.

For airplane food it wasn't bad and it was hot. Remember now, this is my first plane ride so I had nothing else to compare the food to. Anyway after breakfast was served I found I needed to go to the restroom. I don't think I have ever been in a smaller restroom. I had to turn sideways just to get in there. Once in there, there's this little silver thing called a toilet and I'm wondering the whole time, 'who uses this thing!' I did manage to take care of business and squeeze my way out, to find a small line forming. There was a rather large woman in line and I couldn't help to wonder if she'd make it in there. I went back to my seat and this time Oscar let me sit near the window. After a while I forgot all about being on an airplane and just enjoyed the view. The clouds were beautiful and when I looked down below it was like a dream. I could see the outline of lakes and ponds and seeing the mountains from so far up was awesome!! I kept pointing things out to my husband and, yes, I squealed like a two-year old with a new toy. I was having so much fun that the couple in front of us kept smiling and every now and then they'd tell me to look out the window to see something else interesting.

Nearing the end of the flight the captain came over the intercom to tell us to look out our window and glimpse a view of the Hoover Dam. That was an awesome sight. So much so that I asked if we could take one of the tour flights, mind you I was coming to the end of my first ever 4-hour plane ride. Of course Oscar quickly nixed that idea. The attendants had us prepare for landing a few miles from the airport. As the plane began to make its descent; those pesky butterflies came back. But we landed without a hitch. The couple in front of us congratulated me on my first plane ride. I think they were having a little fun at my expense but I didn't care I was back on solid ground.

When we disembarked I remember thanking the attendants, for what

I don't know; but my husband smiled and told them it was my first plane ride and they started clapping. I realized that my knees were a little shaky, but I was fine in no time at all.

We had to go to the baggage claim area to get our luggage; it was entertaining to watch people get their luggage. If you weren't quick enough you had to run to the other side to get your luggage before it seemed to disappear again. HA, I got mine on the first try. After getting the luggage we had to get a taxi to our hotel. I talked the whole time about the airplane ride and asked a million questions. Patient Oscar just smiled and answered them. We spent three days in Vegas and then we had to make the return trip.

It really takes my husband to tell you about the trip home. When we got to the airport I was determined to not let the butterflies invade my serenity. I failed; because the minute that plane took off they came. And to make matters worse we were flying in the dark. Now mind you I know we drive in our cars in the dark but I actually asked my husband how the pilot's going to know which way to go. Instruments and lights were not a part of my thought processes. Anyway going home was different because I got sleepy after a while. So I took what masqueraded as a pillow and tried to find a comfortable way to sleep. At some point along the way the flight attendants served us a snack. I liked flying to Vegas better. All we got going home was a DRINK and a BAG of NUTS! The flight home was uneventful until we ran into some turbulence. I think I was half-asleep when I heard Oscar murmur something about not liking the feel of things. The plane dipped a few times and then the pilot came over the intercom to inform us that we'd run into patch of rough weather, but that we would be out of it soon.

Now there I am, the second time on a plane in my life and I'm patting my husband's hand and telling him, "don't worry honey it's just a little turbulence we'll be alright", and promptly turned back to my somewhat comfortable position to go back to sleep. I think he had a good 10- minute laugh on my account.

When the plane landed in Atlanta we retrieved our luggage and were headed to the car when I asked my husband, "So where are we flying to next year for vacation? This flying thing is cool!" I exclaimed, and he laughed again.

To this day my husband loves to tell the story of my first plane ride. For me it just started to open the door for me to experience many more wonderful things. Now that I have Fresh Start for Women I know without a doubt that I'll be able to go wherever I need to and not be afraid.

Courage...what another beautiful jewel!

Chapter 10 – Communicate & Organize

In December 2001 my good friend Wilbert Scott suggested that I become a member of Toastmasters and invited me to attend one of Big T's club meetings. This is important because this too was God's way of preparing me for the purpose and mission he had for me. All of this came about because of a project we were working on together at church that would have required me to speak in front of people I did not know. I enjoyed being in the background and doing the research or whatever else was needed to accomplish the task before us; as long as I didn't have to be up front any more than was necessary.

<u>I also had a dream of owning my own bakery some day.</u> Of course I'm sure you're wondering how I could do that if I couldn't talk to people. Me too! So I took him up on his offer and attended my first meeting later that month.

Not knowing anyone but Wilbert I thought I would feel intimidated, but was pleasantly surprised. Not only was I not intimidated; the other members welcomed me with smiling faces.

As I watched the activities and saw how everyone supported each other I knew I wanted to join. Of course the food was a plus! After the meeting I went ahead and joined before I changed my mind.

On January 22, 2002 I gave that first speech called an Ice Breaker. I can honestly say that before the day arrived for me to speak I agonized over what I would say. I wrote things down and changed my mind several times.

I tried practicing in front of the mirror and even tried it out on a couple of friends to get their input. Nothing seemed to help those butterflies that were active in my stomach. Up until a few days before I was to speak I didn't even have a title. Then it dawned on me. I'll talk about the Country Girl in the City. From there I was on my way.

I made it through that first speech without doing many of the things I was terrified I would do. Usually I talk too fast or get so tongue-tied that no one understands me, or worse every thought leaves my head; and then I can't wait to slink into the background and hide.

After the speech another experienced Toastmaster had the privilege of evaluating my speech. She thanked me for sharing my story and then complimented me on my strong points. I sometimes refer back to that first evaluation to make sure that I continue to do the things the Toastmaster gave me high marks for and to remind myself of what she told me not to do. One thing she mentioned was to not draw attention to any nervousness I might have when speaking by telling everyone I was nervous. She even complimented me when she reminded me that although I had walked to the lectern with notes, I never used them! That in itself was a huge accomplishment!

After that first speech I couldn't wait to have lunch with my mentor. I already had a topic for my next speech. I'm sure if you ask Wilbert when I'm not around he'll admit that I really took the word mentor to heart and pestered him often to read just one more speech and tell me what he thought.

If you ever have the opportunity to visit a Toastmasters club I promise you'll be ready to join. When you do join be sure to have a mentor. That's what they're there for to help and guide you through your first few speeches. Because of Toastmasters, I realized the dream of owning my own bakery someday. I even had the courage and the confidence to approach my company's regional vice-president and tell him about my business venture.

For about 2 years I provided the cakes for the office birthday celebrations each month. Not only that but my fellow Toastmasters believed in me as well, at one of the meetings they presented me with a beautiful card that I still have. I looked at often for it was filled with well wishes and money to obtain my business license.

I worked out of my home late at night preparing delicious cakes and pies to order. Holidays were my busiest. I no longer bake but that achievement prepared me for Fresh Start for Women because I had to know how to interact with different people and it taught me to take pride in my work.

Thanks to the confidence gained in Toastmasters I joined the drama ministry at church and found myself performing before large audiences. Again God was preparing me for my purpose and mission.

Talk about the behind the scenes' person breaking out!! I'm not through - I joined the Speakers Bureau and had several opportunities to go to various companies and groups to speak. This really got me out of my comfort zone!

I made numerous presentations at Toastmaster conferences and one year I traveled to Charleston, SC to do a 45-minute presentation to the Ford Motor Company's annual secretary/treasurers convention. This was my largest crowd yet to speak before.

Shortly after that I served as chair of the fall conference. This meant I had the responsibility of putting together a team to help put on a conference for which Toastmasters from all over the state of Georgia would attend.

Thanks to these experiences I was able to discover two more beautiful jewels; the ability to **communicate** and **organize**!

Chapter 11 - Faith

My greatest gift and most precious jewel is my faith. I enjoy what I do and one day I know without a doubt that God will make a way for me to do this every day and still be able to take care of my daily living responsibilities. Why faith?

Because it is the one thing that has been tested the most and I'm still here and working as God has directed me. In June of 2006, just two weeks shy of my forty-ninth birthday I received a call at work that sent me rushing to the hospital.

My youngest brother had called the ambulance earlier that morning to have our mom transported to the hospital. I left work a bundle of nerves as my friend, Valrita, drove me to the hospital. I couldn't think straight and prayed and begged God to please let her be all right. When the doctors finally met with us, the news was not good. Mama was in a coma and the prognosis for her to come out of it was very slim. They still needed to run some tests but would meet with us as soon as they had more to report. I remember James asking if it would be okay if we prayed. The doctors nodded and James led us all in prayer. Afterwards the doctors left to continue their work.

I remember sitting in the waiting room trying to stay positive but fearing the worst. You see a few months earlier while taking my mom to the grocery store I noticed how tired she looked and how thin she was. When I asked about it she just said she wasn't eating much because she just didn't have an appetite. When I went home that day I told Oscar I saw death on her and it worried me. Now here we were and it just didn't look good. A few hours later the doctors returned and confirmed my worst fears. Mom had cancer and it had metastasized through her lungs. The machines were doing all the work for her and we would need to make a decision to have the machines removed. It's at that time that my heart plummeted to my stomach.

We made phone calls to her brothers and sisters and agonized over the news we'd been given. We asked for a second opinion and then we asked God. After we'd had a day to come to grips with what we'd been given, we gave permission for the machines to be removed. I spent time massaging her feet. Mama always loved having her feet massaged, so I asked the nurse for some lotion and began to ever so gently rub her feet. Mixed in with the lotion were my tears as I said goodbye to my mom.

All of her children were there when she took her last breath. And so the grieving began. It took over a year for me to see the good in all of this. It wasn't easy and my faith faltered a time or two but I hung on. I cried, I railed, I questioned. I beat myself up because I didn't do something. I was even mad at mama for not taking better care of herself. She was always putting us kids, grandkids and others before her. A tragedy like this can either bring a family closer together or pull them further apart. It'll be three years in a couple of days and I think we're in a holding pattern.

Returning to work was hard after mama died I didn't want to do anything but I knew I had to return to work so I just buried myself more in work. Of course I made more than a few mistakes; a lot more than I normally would on a daily basis. I felt as if I was living in a fog and I wanted and needed to feel alive again. So one day I went into my quiet place and had it out with God.

Boy, no matter what he's still a good listener. I told him I felt cheated and that I was angry with mama, him and me. In the dark I cried deep from my soul and asked him to please keep me strong. I promised him then that I'd always trust his decision and I have faith he'd done what was best for mama.

I was reminded that she didn't suffer, and I was grateful for that but oh how I miss her. Mama taught me a lot. Oscar is fond of saying, "Like mother, like daughter." I take it as a compliment but I also take the lessons from it as well. As much as I love my family, if I don't take care of me I can't take care of them. Mama was stubborn, bullheaded even, very independent when she wanted to be. I can see now that I get that from her.

Mama loved us children without reservation and that's a lesson I'll always keep with me. I'm grateful that before mama passed I had the opportunity to finally tell her about those things she had no clue about. I had to before I started sharing it with the world. I can still feel the hug and hear her say how sorry she was I suffered in silence. I made sure she knew I didn't blame her. I miss her so much but I believe she's proud of the woman I've become.

Through it all my faith is strong and I know without a doubt that there are more jewels waiting for me to reveal.

The Birth of a Purpose & a Mission

Chapter 12 –The Birth

As I said in 2003 God gave me a purpose and a mission. Naturally I knew I could not do this all on my own but I knew I had at least one person in my corner to depend on and help me, my husband Oscar.

You see before it became a reality we'd had numerous discussions about my life. On more than one occasion I expressed the need to do something more than just go to work, come home and do it all over again.

In my own words I said, "I want a life".

To which Oscar asked, "Well what do you want to do?"

I quickly responded that I wanted to help other women who had experienced some of the same things I had. I wanted to encourage them and show them that they didn't have to be defined by their past. I wanted to help them realize the untapped potential inside of them waiting to reveal the gifts God had just for them. Wow! That was a mouthful.

And all Oscar said was "be careful what you ask for".

I remember feeling nervous, excited and overwhelmed all at the same time. Oscar was my rock and encourager every step of the way. In January 2004 I sent out a call to other women interested in helping with this new endeavor. About a dozen women showed up at the Piccadilly Restaurant in South DeKalb Mall. Of the dozen women in attendance that evening three became founding members of the Fresh Start for Women board of directors. What a rush! How exciting! And what a responsibility!

For weeks we met and planned and developed strategies for success.

We finally developed the vision for **Fresh Start for Women, Inc.** – To empower and renew the lives of women spiritually, physically and emotionally. That has since changed to seeing women live successfully in communities free from domestic violence, abuse and sexual assault.

Our mission and purpose would allow us to provide a positive and supportive environment in which women are able to rebuild their self-esteem spiritually, physically and emotionally. We would encourage wiser life choices through education and counseling. We wanted to facilitate the healing process and break the cycle of violence by helping women develop healthy relationships. It was also important that it be faith-based.

We pondered what the meaning would be for the first 2 words Fresh Start. Late into the night Oscar and I discussed it and this is what we settled on and why.

Friendship – No man or woman is an island but it is important to understand the meaning of friendship. We wanted to make sure women could make an informed decision when it comes to choosing friends and giving their friendship in return.

Restoration – Hurt people need to be restored. They need to know that they matter.

Encouragement – Without encouragement how can you reach your highest potential? We wanted to offer encouragement not criticism.

Sharing – The gift of sharing allows us to be a part of each other's lives in a way that is positive and beneficial.

Helping – We offer assistance with our hearts, mind and spirit.

Sacrificing – Giving out of our need so that others may have.

Trust – Faith and belief in the goodness of mankind.

Achievement – Setting and reaching goals for a fulfilling life.

Realization – Bring hopes and dreams to reality.

Truth – Sharing God's Word and the power it holds.

After months of planning we were ready to conduct the first program. The inaugural program was a huge success! This first program was conducted over 4 consecutive Saturdays. We welcomed five beautiful women to the program. We invited them to be prepared with an open heart and mind, ready and willing to receive the gift of love and respect. We told them to be in expectation of becoming empowered to make a change in their circumstances.

It all began with a trip to the Fresh Start Spa, where the women were treated to a morning of pampering provided by board members and volunteers. Board member Sharon Battle had received permission to use the office where she worked to conduct the program. We arrived early on that first day and transformed the meeting room into the Fresh Star Spa. We had scented candles and soft music playing in the background. We wanted to give them a feeling of being in their own private place. On hand were Donna Shaw with her basic manicures and pedicures and Joan Mockalis with an introduction to better skin care. Other volunteers provided simple massages. We used this day to give the women a chance to get comfortable with us and in turn be willing to open up.

We had gift bags waiting for them with all kinds of goodies including journals. The journals we encouraged them to personalize by decorating them. We also allowed time for them to write in their new journals what they were feeling at that moment. Throughout the program time was set aside for these quiet moments of reflection. Donna shared with them the benefits of recording their thoughts and feelings as they prepared to embark on their Fresh Start journey. During their Spa experience one woman commented, "I am overwhelmed to have other women volunteer their time to pamper me".

We weren't looking for any major changes after just one day, but to see women smiling because someone was taking care of them gave us hope and encouragement that we were on the right tract. The following Saturday the real work began. It opened with me sharing my story. It wasn't a pity party, oh no. I wanted the women to know that I had once walked in their shoes and understood that those shoes could have you doubting yourself and not trusting others. Just by opening up my life to them they were able to open up as well and in the process encourage and support each other.

I'll never forget the Saturday in which we talked about positive affirmations. At first it was difficult for the women to come up with positive things about themselves. With some gentle prodding, some very powerful statements emerged. Some of them were:

I am Beautiful

I am Love

I am a Good Mother

I am a Good Communicator

I am a Survivor

I am a Conqueror

I am Smart

I am God's Child

I am Sexy

I am Strong

I am Healed

These were just a few of the statements made. Since that time we've taken these statements placed them on cards and now do what we call an Affirmation Circle. We take the cards turn them over and then one by one the women pull a card. You don't know what the card says until you turn it over. In the 3 years since we've been doing it this way, it has never failed to amaze us that the women always manage to pull just exactly what they need!

It was in this same session that we pulled out magazines, scissors, clue and other decorations and gave the women a poster board to design a collage depicting the desires they had for themselves for the next 3 – 5 years. As a matter of fact we all did one. Me I did it for Fresh Start for Women. Once the collages were completed we wouldn't let them take the collages home because we had a surprise for them. The following Saturday would be the last and so we wanted them to be able to take the collages home and hang them up so they could see them every day. We wanted it to be visible encouragement for them to strive for whatever it is they had placed on the collage.

When the final Saturday arrived the women were welcomed into the meeting room, this time with the office decorated for a party. Balloons, glitter and a celebratory lunch were also provided. The women were greeted with their collages framed and ready to be hung up. This first program culminated with the women sharing not only their experiences over the past 4 weeks but also their personally designed collage of their future dreams and goals. One woman remarked, "I have learned to stop beating myself up with a hammer but to use a feather instead". This comment elicited tears and cheers from everyone!

Having gained the confidence to let go those things they no longer wished to hold onto, the women released them into God's hands in a moving ceremony we called 'The Balloon Release' Amid the tears were tons of hugs and kisses and congratulations on the completion of the first phase of their new Fresh Start journey.

Since that first program we've conducted several others. We even turned the program into a weekend retreat in which participants spent an entire weekend focused on self-evaluation and mutual support. Two years later we expanded the program to eight weeks, which, we offer to women currently residing in the shelter environment. The original program is now conducted as a weekend retreat filled with surprises for all! Plans are in the works to expand even further and offer so much more, including housing and life coaching.

Fresh Start for Women is the result of my journey to a Fresh Start. The journey has brought me through some very trying times but there have been many joys along the way as well. All of it is a part of the person I am so I am now able to look at my faults, flaws, victories and failures and still love myself. There were many times I could have given up but at my worst the God in me made me stand till he'd finished a work in me.

No He's not done with me and I look forward to what's ahead with excitement. I like to tell people that the months leading up to the first program were my final labor pains for the birth of Fresh Start for Women into the world. A couple of years later another birth happened.

Chapter 13 – Another Birth

In 2006 we included a program for teen girls called "**You Are a Precious Jewel**".

"You Are a Precious Jewel" was the brainchild of then Board President Donna Shaw, who had expressed a desire to have a positive impact on the lives of young girls. It was also important to me because of the 23 grandchildren I had at the time 9 were girls. My greatest desire was to do my best to prevent my granddaughters and anyone else's daughter from going through what I'd experienced. So we designed a program with our young charges in mind. It was presented as an all day workshop where we discussed peer pressure, goal setting and self-esteem.

That first workshop was an eye-opener for me! I never realized just how much pressure our teens girls are faced with everyday. To hear their thoughts about sex and fitting in made my heart bleed. One young lady admitted she was so desperate to fit in that she lied about her age. So much so that when she got hurt while playing and had to go to the emergency room when asked how old she was she said 15. She was actually 13 at the time. She said she felt it was the only way to be accepted in the neighborhood so somewhere along the way she began to believe the lie. It took her mother showing her the birth certificate for the truth to hit home.

How sad and heartbreaking to have young girls 13 – 17 under such pressure! They should have been concentrating on their education, developing healthy relationships, learning how to set boundaries and to learn and discover their own gifts and talents. What we learned that day was just the tip of the iceberg but it made me acutely aware that my experiences at 13 could also be used with these teens to speak encouragement and support.

I'll never forget the first time I was invited to speak to a group of girls age 12 – 14 and while sharing my story one young lady asked

– so what were you wearing? The girls were all seated on the floor in a circle in front of me. I took that opportunity to get down in the circle with them and making eye contact with each girl I said" sweetheart – it doesn't matter if I didn't have a stitch of clothes on – No means No! Here I was having this conversation with 12, 13 and 14 year old girls and I could tell from the body language of many that some serious conversations needed to be had with someone more qualified than me. I expressed my concerns to the person in charge and got assurances that they would follow-up. It was later that I learned my concerns were valid. Thank God I wasn't ashamed or I could have missed an opportunity to help someone in need. Sometimes all it takes is the right words to move mountains.

A year later with God's guidance the program was expanded into a 12-week program. This expanded program offers teens a positive and supportive environment in which they feel comfortable in discussing issues such as peer pressure, teen violence, domestic violence, abuse and its effects on teens. Through the program teens are taught to use the arts (dance, drama, drawing/painting and music) as a means of expressing their concerns in a positive manner. We are looking forward to partnering with other groups to provide ongoing mentoring and support for each of the participants. Helping teen girls to recognize just how important they are to God is making an impact. We tell them all the time that they are Precious Jewels. For they are:

Joy in God's Eyes

Enriched with His Grace

Wrapped in His Mercy

Embraced by His Courage

Loved Divinely

It is in this setting that I share my experiences at the age of 13 and the ramifications of them. I want to talk to and with them not at them. It is my desire to inspire them to reach for the stars and not be defined by other's opinions. This addition to the Fresh Start for Women program was definitely the right thing to do. I guess my husband Oscar was right you do have to be careful what you ask for.

Fresh Start for Women and You Are a Precious Jewel are the two babies that God gave me as a result of the life I've led. I'm their mother and my husband Oscar is their father. How many people do you know who can proudly say that there's no part of their lives they care to change? It's not an easy statement to make but for me the good the bad and the indifferent circumstances of my life have all played an important role in shaping the person I am today. Proudly I proclaim that the purpose and mission God gave me in 2003 is here!

Journey to a Fresh Start

My wedding day! The day I married the voice and we became one.

My little Angels!

852513

All grown up & members of the wedding

The very first Fresh Start for Women program. The women were presented with gift bags filled with all kinds of goodies including the journals they would decorate. The final day saw them releasing their concerns into God's hands!

The first "Precious Jewel" program was conducted at a local library.

Here are the trees from which I sprouted.

Words from My Best Friend

In writing this book I asked my best friend and husband to write a few words to share with my audience. This is what he wrote:

This world (Satan's kingdom) is not built on love and caring. It is built on love of vanity, selfishness, enviousness and strife. Out of these things awful things are inflicted upon men and women. Abuse, injury and death are everyday occurrences. Society has accepted by the handling of the heart, these occurrences. This condition leads to loss of love and caring toward one another.

 Fear reigns throughout the world. The weak are preyed on daily. Only the strong survive is the chant. Laws were put in effect, but the law does not change the heart of men. What it did was create another side of the same coin, kill or be killed, legally. Laws were enacted to punish crimes, but this did not stop man's treatment of man.

Then "Jesus Christ" came into the world and showed us a better way, a way of strength. He showed us a way of exacting power over the enemy. That way is "Love". This is <u>True</u> <u>Power</u>. 'Love your enemy, bless those that curse you.' Pray for them that despitefully use you. Jesus showed us the way to another world, a world of righteousness, which was and did change man and his perceptions.

The world sees this as weak, but this is <u>True Power</u>, for God is Love and he that does not love has never known him or seen him. In order to obtain <u>True</u> <u>Power</u>, you must be born again out of the flesh into the spirit, thereby, gaining power over the works of the flesh. Creating a new <u>YOU</u>! Hallelujah!!!

We cannot receive the power until we are born again and have received the Holy Ghost. Then there abides Faith, Hope & Charity (Love) and the greatest of these is Charity (Love). Then and only then can we have strength to: Forgive, Bless, and Change our situations in life, because we have the Holy Ghost to Lead, Guide and Comfort us.

Praise God!!

Finally know this, when you meet a person that does a good deed or an act of love and kindness, then God is there.

As Co-founder and spiritual counselor for **Fresh Start for Women, Inc.,** my husband wrote the following two poems. This first poem is quite appropriate when you need additional encouragement. Remember in chapter 9 this jewel was revealed to me. It was first presented at one of our retreats in 2006.

Courage

It takes courage to live
It takes no courage to die
It takes courage to feel
It takes courage to fly

If I live, feel, fly, or die
Let it be with courage
It takes courage to face you fears
It takes courage to live

It takes courage to stand-up and hear
It takes courage to heal
Do I live, Do I heal, Do I fear or
Do I hear?

When I am lonely, when I cannot face me
It takes courage to stand and see
Who I am, how I came to be
Then and only then do I see the power of Thee

By Thee O God is my courage given
By thy spirit and strength am I sustained
By Thee O Lord am I living
By Thee O Lord, I am a man or woman.

Does Love Suppose to Hurt

Where is this place I find myself?
Did I take a wrong turn somewhere?
I knew where I was going when I left
I must have passed it, when I got there.

Strange as it may seem
I don't know what love is.
I thought I did, I think I know what it means.
I love someone, is it suppose to kill?
Does love suppose to hurt?

I woke up one day and thought it was night.
The sun was supposed to shine.
Something is just not right.
Have I lost my mind?
Does love suppose to hurt?

The hand that caressed me with tenderness & care,
Now bludgeons me with pain.
The mouth that kissed me can only swear.
Have I lost what I thought I gained?
Does love suppose to hurt?

Do I leave? And do I dare?
My mind says go, my heart says stay.
I'm caught in a place, I know not where.
Dear God help me find my way.
Does love suppose to hurt?

Author's Note

Each day God reveals many more new truths to me. It's amazing how much there is to learn and so I never want to stop learning. As long as I'm learning I'm also able to help someone else. Should a time come that I stop learning then I pray it's because God is calling me home.

Each day I wake with a prayer of thanksgiving and gratitude, for I know it is not because of anything I've done that I do. It is all because of God's Mercy and His Grace and the Sacrifice of His Son Jesus Christ. I gladly share of myself faults and flaws, just as God desired. May your life be filled with God's Love. And I implore you come on let today be the beginning of your Journey to a Fresh Start.

About the Author

Having spent more than 16 years in corporate America Janice Pettigrew began to question her purpose in life. Janice always felt there was more to it than just earning a paycheck and began to earnestly explore avenues of fulfillment.

This quest led her to using the communication and leadership skills developed through Toastmasters to begin speaking in public about her experiences as a victim of domestic violence, abuse and rape.

During these talks she met women of all ages and races who had similar experiences and a common thread. Many found that they were stalled, unable to move forward and afraid to look back, caught up in a grip too strong to break on their own. Understanding the toll these experiences can take on a woman's self-esteem Janice saw a need to have a place that was safe, loving, and positive for victims of domestic violence to reconnect with their inner beauty.

With the support and guidance of husband and co-founder Minister Oscar Pettigrew, Jr., the nonprofit organization Fresh Start for Women, Inc. was born dedicated to rebuilding self-esteem in women spiritually, physically and emotionally.

Janice Pettigrew is a powerful inspirational and motivational speaker and facilitator demonstrating to women the endless possibilities that still await them. Janice uses her experiences as examples of the healing powers of acceptance, understanding and forgiveness and encourages women to not be defined by their circumstances.

Armed with love, patience, tears and smiles, she along with dedicated professionals and volunteers gently guide women through their journey of self-evaluation on the road to rediscovering their hopes and dreams.

Janice Pettigrew is the mother of 2 (stepmom) to 4 and grandmother of 26. When not working with Fresh Start for Women, Janice enjoys reading and baking goodies for her grandchildren.

For Information on booking Janice Pettigrew
for a speaking engagement

Or

To send correspondence you may write to her at:

P O Box 370681

Decatur, GA 30037

Or Email: janicepettigrew@gmail.com

www.ingramcontent.com/pod-product-compliance
Lightning Source LLC
Chambersburg PA
CBHW071422040426
42445CB00012BA/1265